Using Benefit-Cost Review in Mitigation Planning

State and Local Mitigation Planning
How-To Guide Number Five
FEMA 386-5 *May 2007*

U.S. Department of Homeland Security
500 C Street, SW
Washington, DC 20472

TABLE OF CONTENTS

The **Disaster Mitigation Act of 2000** (DMA 2000) provides an opportunity for States, Tribal governments, and local jurisdictions to significantly reduce their vulnerability to natural hazards. It also allows them to streamline the receipt and use of Federal disaster assistance through pre-disaster hazard mitigation planning. DMA 2000 places new emphasis on State, Tribal, and local mitigation planning by requiring these entities to develop and submit mitigation plans as a condition of receiving various types of pre- and post-disaster assistance (such as the Pre-Disaster Mitigation [PDM] program and the Hazard Mitigation Grant Program [HMGP]) under the Stafford Act.

On February 26, 2002, the Department of Homeland Security's Federal Emergency Management Agency (FEMA) published an **Interim Final Rule** (the Rule) to implement the mitigation planning requirements of DMA 2000. The Rule outlines the requirements for State, Tribal and local mitigation plans.

FEMA has developed a series of guides, called the **Mitigation Planning "How-To" Guides**, to provide State, Tribal, and local governments with easy-to-understand information needed to initiate and maintain a hazard mitigation planning process and meet the requirements of the Rule. The guides can be ordered free of cost by calling 1-800-480-2520, or they can be downloaded from http://www.fema.gov/plan/mitplanning/planning_resources.shtm#1.

The first four How-To Guides are known as the "core four" guides. They provide the basic instructions for preparing a natural hazard mitigation plan. They are:

- *Getting Started: Building Support for Mitigation Planning* (FEMA 386-1)

- *Understanding Your Risks: Identifying Hazards and Estimating Losses* (FEMA 386-2)

- *Developing the Mitigation Plan: Identifying Mitigation Actions and Implementation Strategies* (FEMA 386-3)

- *Bringing the Plan to Life: Implementing the Hazard Mitigation Plan* (FEMA 386-4)

This How-To Guide, Using Benefit-Cost Review in Mitigation Planning (FEMA 386-5), supplements FEMA 386-3 and focuses on guidance for using Benefit-Cost Review when prioritizing mitigation actions in a hazard mitigation plan.

About This Document

Purpose

The purpose of a mitigation plan is to reduce the community's vulnerability to hazards. After assessing its risks, a community may consider many mitigation options. However, due to monetary as well as other limitations, it is often impossible to implement all mitigation actions. Hence, the Planning Team needs to select the most cost-effective actions for implementation first, not only to use resources efficiently, but to make a realistic start toward mitigating risks.

The Rule supports the principle of cost-effectiveness by requiring hazard mitigation plans to have an action plan that includes a prioritization process that demonstrates a special emphasis on maximization of benefits over costs. The requirement states:

> *The mitigation strategy section shall include] an action plan describing how the actions identified in section (c)(3)(ii) will be prioritized, implemented, and administered by the local jurisdiction. Prioritization shall include a special emphasis on the extent to which benefits are maximized according to a cost benefit review of the proposed projects and their associated costs. [§201.6(c)(3)(iii)]*

The purpose of this guide is to help local jurisdictions understand how to apply the concepts of Benefit-Cost Review to the prioritization of mitigation actions, and thereby meet the requirement of the Rule.

Benefit-Cost Review vs. Benefit-Cost Analysis

The Benefit-Cost Review for mitigation planning differs from the benefit-cost analysis (BCA) used for specific projects. BCA is a method for determining the potential positive effects of a mitigation action and comparing them to the cost of the action. To assess and demonstrate the cost-effectiveness of mitigation actions, FEMA has developed a suite of BCA software, including hazard-specific modules. The analysis determines whether a mitigation project is technically cost-effective.

The principle behind the BCA is that the benefit of an action is a reduction in future damages. The Benefit-Cost Review method described in this guide is based on the same principle, but this guide does NOT explain how to conduct a BCA. DMA 2000 does not require hazard mitigation plans to include BCAs for specific projects.

A Benefit-Cost Review can satisfy the DMA 2000 requirements even if it is relatively simple. Remember that a Benefit-Cost Review can be broad and need not be complex. It needs to be comprehensive so that it covers monetary as well as non-monetary costs and benefits associated with each action. Some projects can be extremely cost-effective but not as beneficial for the community at large. The Planning Team should think through a wide variety of questions, such as: How many people will benefit from the action? How large an area is impacted? How critical are the facilities that benefit from the action (e.g., is it more beneficial to protect the fire station than the administrative building, even though it costs more)? Environmentally, does it make sense to do this project for the overall community?

A hazard mitigation plan must demonstrate that a process was employed that emphasized a review of costs and benefits when prioritizing the mitigation actions. This requirement allows the Planning Team flexibility in determining which method to use. Four methods are described in this document, ranging from qualitative to more quantitative. These examples are intended to be illustrative of acceptable processes, but do not cover all possible methods that are approvable under DMA 2000.

How to Use This How-To Guide

The Rule states, "The mitigation strategy shall include a section that identifies and analyzes a comprehensive range of mitigation actions." However, no specific methodology for the analysis is specified or required. FEMA 386-3 discusses some ways to conduct an analysis. This How-To Guide, Using Benefit-Cost Review in Mitigation Planning (FEMA 386-5), provides methods and examples to review benefits and costs, prioritize actions and document the entire process.

This guide is organized as follows:

Part 1 - Review Benefits and Costs – This section explains how to review benefits and costs for each action.

Part 2 A - Prioritize Actions – Qualitative Methods – This section provides two qualitative methods to prioritize actions (Methods A and B).

Part 2 B - Prioritize Actions – Quantitative Methods – This section provides two quantitative methods to prioritize actions (Methods C and D).

Part 3 - Document the Review and Prioritization Process – This section discusses documentation of the Benefit-Cost Review process in the plan to meet DMA 2000 requirements.

Worksheets (Review Tools) like the ones in Part 1 can be used to summarize the costs and benefits. After the review of benefits and costs for each action, the Planning Team will be able to prioritize the actions.

They can then use one of the four methods (A to D), which range from simple to complex. See Figure 1 for an illustration of how to use this guide. Blank worksheets are included in Appendix A, Exhibits. The worksheets can be duplicated and used to record the progress of prioritizing mitigation actions for the hazard mitigation plan.

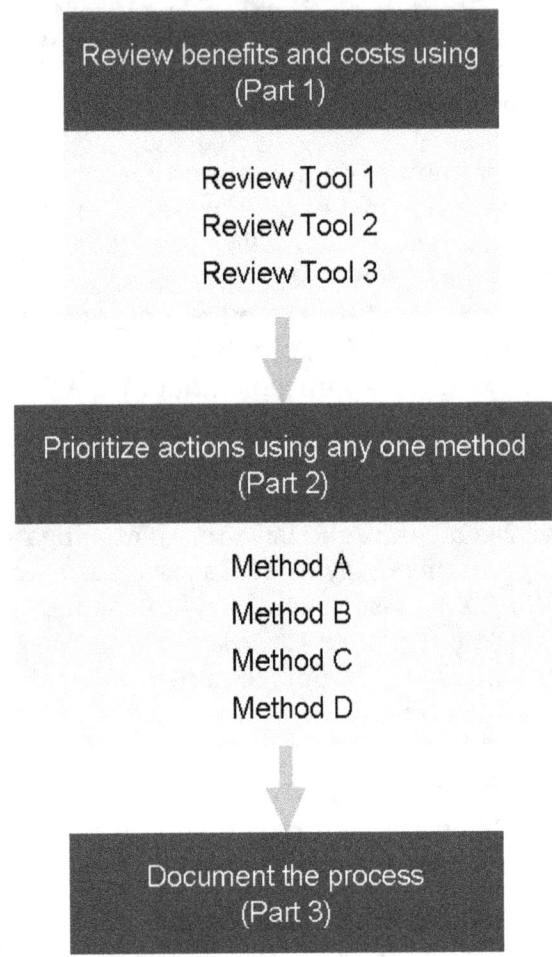

Figure 1. How to Use This How-To Guide

Therefore, a hazard mitigation plan will meet the requirements of the Rule by:

- Using Review Tools 1, 2, and 3 from Part 1,

- Using any one prioritization method from Part 2 (Method A, B, C, or D), and

- Documenting the process (as described in Part 3).

PART 1: REVIEW BENEFITS AND COSTS

To assess the measurable and non-measurable benefits and costs associated with each action, use Review Tools 1, 2, and 3. Then, summarize the analysis of each action's benefits and costs and use this review later when prioritizing the actions.

Review Tool 1: Measuring Vulnerability Before and After Mitigation

Action: _____

Vulnerability	Before the Action is implemented*	After the Action is implemented*	Difference
Number of people affected by the hazard			
Area affected (acreage) by the hazard			
Number of properties affected by the hazard			
Property damage (amount in $)			
Loss of use (number of properties/physical assets [e.g., bridges] in number of days)			
Loss of life (number of people)			
Injury (number of people)			
**			

*Include measurable items, where possible, based on experience, professional estimate, or judgment.
**Add more categories of risk as appropriate for the specific community's plan.

Sample Exhibit 1: Measuring Vulnerability Before and After Mitigation
(Exhibit 1 shows Review Tool 1 filled out for one action)

Action: Floodproof 10 businesses in the downtown area

Vulnerability	Before the Action is implemented	After the Action is implemented	Difference
Number of people affected by the hazard	Almost entire community (because downtown is affected)	Same as before but they will be less affected if businesses are able to remain open	Less impact
Area affected (acreage) by the hazard	1 acre	1 acre	Area still affected but less impact
Number of properties affected by the hazard	15	5	10
Property damage (amount in $)	$100,000 every year	$10,000 every year	$90,000 every year
Loss of use (number of properties/physical assets [e.g., bridges] in number of days)	10 properties for 5 days every year	0	Completely eliminated
Loss of life (number of people)	2 every 20 years	1 every 20 years	Reduced by half
Injury (number of people)	0	0	0

PART 1: REVIEW BENEFITS AND COSTS

A simple listing of other costs and benefits (that do not fit into the quantitative format of Review Tool 1) can supplement Review Tool 1, as shown in Review Tools 2 and 3. Fill out as many items as possible.

Review Tool 2: Benefits

Action: _____

Benefits
Risk reduction (short- or long-term)
If other community goals are achieved, explain
If easy to implement, explain
If funding is available, explain
If politically/socially acceptable, explain

Sample Exhibit 2: Benefits

Action: Floodproof 10 businesses in the downtown area

Benefits
City's cost to repair flooded properties reduced by 80%; approximate saving of $5,000 per year
Flooding problem in downtown area solved for the long-term; community's problem of business interruption solved
Federal grants like Flood Mitigation Assistance (FMA) and PDM can be applied for to implement the proposed floodproofing
Will help improve CRS rating in the long term (so entire community's flood insurance premium will be reduced)
More than half the members of the City Council are opposed to buy-outs; it might be easier to get their support for an alternative to buy-outs

Review Tool 3: Costs

Action: _____

Costs*
Construction cost (amount in $)
Programming cost (amount in $, # of people needed to administer)
Time needed to implement
If unfair to a certain social group, explain
If there is public/political opposition, explain
If there are any adverse effects on the environment, explain

*If precise costs are not available, use costs based on experience, professional estimate, or judgment.

Sample Exhibit 3: Costs

Action: Floodproof 10 businesses in the downtown area

Costs
Floodproofing cost = $10,000 X 10 = $100,000
Need at least 3 people to administer (after technical assistance from the State)
Need a year to implement

PART 1: REVIEW BENEFITS AND COSTS

After reviewing benefits and costs for all the actions using the Review Tools, go on to prioritize the actions. Note that there are many ways of prioritizing actions; however, DMA 2000 mandates an emphasis on Benefit-Cost Review as part of the prioritization process. Directly linking the prioritization process to the Benefit-Cost Review clearly shows that costs and benefits were emphasized. Therefore, when the review of benefits and costs of actions in Part 1 is used to prioritize the actions using one of the methods from Part 2, the process meets DMA 2000 requirements.

PART 2A: PRIORITIZE ACTIONS - QUALITATIVE METHODS

Based on the review completed in Part 1, use Part 2 to prioritize or rank the actions.

The two qualitative methods described in this section rely on a holistic response or common sense ranking. The two quantitative approaches in Part 2B rely more on comparative analysis that can be translated into mathematical scores. When the number of actions is relatively small, a subjective or qualitative process may be used. The greater the number of actions, the more likely it is that a more quantitative approach will be useful in assigning priority.

Method A: Simple Listing

The qualitative method described below helps the Planning Team judge the priorities of actions based on perceived pros and cons (i.e., benefits and costs).

The method is best used when it is not possible, or appropriate, to identify a quantitative measure of benefits and costs. Each action can have a unique advantage or disadvantage that can subsequently be used for prioritization.

Using this method ensures that special emphasis is given to Benefit-Cost Review by categorizing prioritization criteria (e.g., ease of implementation, technical effectiveness) as either benefits or costs.

Step 1: List identified actions

For each hazard, list the actions identified earlier in the plan.

Step 2: Identify benefits and costs

Identify all expected benefits (i.e., positive effects) and costs (i.e., perceived obstacles) of the actions and write these down in the benefits and costs columns, respectively. Use Review Tools 1, 2, and 3 (see Exhibits 1, 2, and 3) from Part 1.

Step 3: Assign priority

As a result of the Benefit-Cost Review, the Planning Team assigns a priority to each action. Priority can be expressed in many ways, such as:

- High, medium, low, accompanied by an explanation of what each term means.

- Priority 1, Priority 2, etc.

- Immediate, short-term, and long-term, accompanied by an explanation of what each category means (e.g., immediate = within a month, short-term = within 6 months, long-term = within 2 years).

Sample Exhibit 4: Prioritization by Listing Benefits and Costs

Actions	Benefits (Pros)	Costs (Cons)	Priority
Floodproof 10 businesses in the downtown area	- Avoidance of 1 loss of life every 20 years (casualties reduced by half) - Saving of $90,000 in private damages and $5,000 in public cost - Loss of use of 10 downtown businesses completely eliminated - Community's problem of business interruption solved - Federal grants like FMA and PDM can be applied for to implement the proposed floodproofing - Will help improve CRS rating in the long term (so entire community's flood insurance premium will be reduced) - More than half the members of the City Council are opposed to buy-outs; it might be easier to get their support for an alternative to buy-outs	- Floodproofing cost = $10,000 X 10 = $100,000 - Need at least 3 people to administer (after obtaining technical assistance from the State) - Need a year to implement	High (Priority no. 1)
Build safe rooms for a neighborhood of 50 homes without basements	- Avoidance of 5 lives lost every 20 years (casualties reduced by half) - Public and political support for mitigating this hazard exists (due to regular recurrence of tornadoes)	- City will share 50% of the cost per existing home = $2,000 X 50 = $100,000 - Administrative cost per home = $1,000 X 50 = $50,000 - Need 3 years to complete - Tornadoes are unpredictable; they may never strike this exact area again	Medium (Priority no. 2)
Broadcast educational video on local channel on hazard mitigation	- Local channel might be willing to broadcast free of cost - Publicity would spread awareness about mitigation methods as well as what to do in an emergency	- Cost of preparing video = $5,000 - Only 5% of population might notice the broadcast - Only 5% of that 5% might actually consider acting on individual mitigation methods	Low (Priority no. 3)

PART 2A: PRIORITIZE ACTIONS - QUALITATIVE METHODS

Method B: Relative Rating

A second approach is to assign relative scores to the actions based on qualitative factors. By rating costs and benefits as High, Medium, and Low, this method clearly emphasizes the Benefit-Cost Review. Exhibit 5 uses a set of factors commonly called STAPLEE, which stands for **S**ocial, **T**echnical, **A**dministrative, **P**olitical, **L**egal, **E**conomic, and **E**nvironmental factors. They are typically used for evaluating planning alternatives. For details on using STAPLEE, refer to FEMA 386-3.

Sample Exhibit 5: Prioritization Using STAPLEE and Qualitative Scores

Actions → / Criteria ↓	Floodproof 10 properties in the downtown area		Build safe rooms in a neighborhood of 50 homes without basements		Broadcast educational video about hazard mitigation on local channel	
	Cost	**Benefit**	**Cost**	**Benefit**	**Cost**	**Benefit**
Social	–	–	L	–	–	–
Technical	M	H	M	M	L	L
Administrative	M	–	M	–	L	–
Political	–	L	–	H	–	–
Legal	–	–	–	–	–	–
Economic	M	H	H	–	–	–
Environmental	–	–	–	–	–	–
Priority	High (priority 1)		Medium (priority 2)		Low (priority 3)	

Definition of rating scale: H=High, M=Medium, L=Low, - None/Not applicable

Use the Review Tools completed in Part 1 to help rate the costs and benefits. For help on how to rank High, Medium, Low, None, or NA, see the explanation about STAPLEE in FEMA 386-3.

PART 2B: PRIORITIZE ACTIONS - QUANTITATIVE METHODS

Quantitative methods typically assign numerical values to concepts like high, medium, and low. The Planning Team needs to review the scores and make sure they make sense.

Method C: Simple Score

A simple way of using scores based on the STAPLEE criteria is shown in Exhibit 6. After the table is completed, the scores can be added to determine priority.

Sample Exhibit 6: Prioritization Using STAPLEE and Simple Scores

Actions → Criteria ↓	Floodproof 10 properties in the downtown area		Build safe rooms in a neighborhood of 50 homes without basements		Broadcast educational video about hazard mitigation on local channel	
	Cost	**Benefit**	**Cost**	**Benefit**	**Cost**	**Benefit**
Social	0	1	-1	1	0	0
Technical	-1	2	-1	2	-1	1
Administrative	-1	0	-1	0	-1	0
Political	0	1	0	1	0	0
Legal	0	0	0	0	0	0
Economic	-1	2	-1	0	0	0
Environmental	0	0	0	0	0	0
Sub-total of cost/benefit	-3	6	-4	4	-2	1
Total Score	-3+6 = 3		-4+4 = 0		-2+1 = -1	
Priority	No. 1		No. 2		No. 3	

Definition of rating scale: 2=Very beneficial, 1=Favorable, 0=None/Not applicable, -1=Not Favorable

The Planning Team should be careful when assigning criteria, scores, and weights to avoid the problem inherent in comparing different types of actions. In the example above, the scores allowed the participants to objectively compare the various actions. The weakness of such a simple method is that very different kinds of actions may score similarly, and if not given qualitative consideration (a common-sense check), may yield a questionable ranking. In this example, the safe-room action's total score is very low compared to the floodproofing action, but the Relative Rating method (Method B in Part 2A) showed that for floodproofing and safe rooms, the actions were similar in how their benefits measured up against the costs, and for both actions the benefits exceeded the costs. The Simple Score method shown above, however, results in a greater difference in the final priority scores (3 vs. 0), indicating a large difference in these actions' cost-effectiveness. A formal Benefit-Cost Analysis for each project would verify whether this large difference is accurate, although it is not required for the plan.

Method D: Weighted Score

As noted in the Simple Score method (Method C), a common-sense adjustment may be necessary to adapt the prioritization to the plan. The weighted score method attempts to compensate for the limitations of the Simple Score method by adding emphasis to those factors judged to be more important.

An example of weighted scores using STAPLEE follows.

Sample Exhibit 7: Prioritization Using STAPLEE and Weighted Scores

Actions → Criteria ↓	Floodproof 10 properties in the downtown		Build safe rooms in a neighborhood of 50 homes without basements		Broadcast educational video about hazard mitigation on local channel	
	Cost	**Benefit**	**Cost**	**Benefit**	**Cost**	**Benefit**
Social (weight = 1)	0	1	-1	1	0	0
Technical (weight = 2)	-1x2=-2	2x2=4	-1x2=-2	2x2=4	-1x2=-2	1x2=2
Administrative (weight = 1)	-1	0	-1	0	-1	0
Political (weight = 1)	0	1	0	1	0	0
Legal (weight = 1)	0	0	0	0	0	0
Economic (weight = 2)	-1x2=-2	2x2=4	-1x2=-2	0	0	0
Environmental (weight = 1)	0	0	0	0	0	0
Sub-total of cost/benefit	-5	10	-6	6	-3	2
Total Score	-5+10 = 5		-6+6 = 0		-3+2 = -1	
Priority	No. 1		No. 2		No. 3	

Definition of rating scale: 2=Very beneficial, 1=Favorable,
0=None/Not applicable, -1=Not Favorable

Assigning weights to some factors over others can become challenging for the Planning Team. Local knowledge and values should guide the process to achieve the priorities most appropriate for the local situation.

PART 3: DOCUMENT THE REVIEW AND PRIORITIZATION PROCESS

Remember to document in the plan the Benefit-Cost Review process and prioritization method used. Include the Review Tools and prioritization worksheets from this How-To Guide in the plan. Clearly explain how the scores and priorities were assigned.

Be sure to explicitly state that Benefit-Cost Review was **emphasized** in the prioritization process. Using the Review Tools and one of the methods for prioritization from this guide ensures the emphasis on the maximization of benefits over costs. This approach demonstrates that the actions are being evaluated in terms of their pros and cons, which are represented as costs and benefits.

The intention of DMA 2000 is for the hazard mitigation plan to be useful and unique for each community; therefore, an impartial review and ranking of the mitigation actions is key. It is not so important which method is used, but rather that the method chosen is logical and clearly documented.

Remember that the Benefit-Cost Review is an important element of the community's hazard mitigation plan. Keep it simple, and focus on your community's needs and values.

Appendix A

Exhibits

Exhibit 1: Measuring Vulnerability Before and After Mitigation

Action: _____

Vulnerability	Before the Action is implemented*	After the Action is implemented*	Difference
Number of people affected by the hazard			
Area affected (acreage) by the hazard			
Number of properties affected by the hazard			
Property damage (amount in $)			
Loss of use (number of properties/physical assets [e.g., bridges] in number of days)			
Loss of life (number of people)			
Injury (number of people)			
**			

*Include measurable items, where possible, based on experience, professional estimate, or judgment.
**Add more categories of risk as appropriate for the specific community's plan.

Exhibit 2: Benefits

Action: _____

Benefits
Risk reduction (short- or long-term)
If other community goals are achieved, explain
If easy to implement, explain
If funding is available, explain
If politically/socially acceptable, explain

Exhibit 3: Costs

Action: _____

Costs*
Construction cost (amount in $)
Programming cost (amount in $, # of people needed to administer)
Time needed to implement
If unfair to a certain social group, explain
If there is public/political opposition, explain
If there are any adverse effects on the environment, explain

*If precise costs are not available, use costs based on experience, professional estimate, or judgment.

Exhibit 4: Prioritization by Listing Benefits and Costs

Actions	Benefits (Pros)	Costs (Cons)	Priority

Exhibit 5: Prioritization Using STAPLEE and Qualitative Scores

Actions → Criteria ↓	Cost	Benefit	Cost	Benefit	Cost	Benefit
Social						
Technical						
Administrative						
Political						
Legal						
Economic						
Environmental						
Priority						

Definition of rating scale: _____

Exhibit 6: Prioritization Using STAPLEE and Simple Scores

Actions → Criteria ↓	Cost	Benefit	Cost	Benefit	Cost	Benefit
Social						
Technical						
Administrative						
Political						
Legal						
Economic						
Environmental						
Sub-total of cost/benefit						
Total Score						
Priority						

Definition of rating scale: _____

Exhibit 7: Prioritization Using STAPLEE and Weighted Scores

Actions → Criteria ↓	Cost	Benefit	Cost	Benefit	Cost	Benefit
Social (weight = __)						
Technical (weight = __)						
Administrative (weight = __)						
Political (weight = __)						
Legal (weight = __)						
Economic (weight = __)						
Environmental (weight = __)						
Sub-total of cost/benefit						
Total Score						
Priority						

Definition of rating scale: _____